JAMES M. KOUZES | BARRY Z. POSNER

LPI

Leadership Practices Inventory

FOURTH EDITION

DEVELOPMENT PLANNER

Pfeiffer™
An Imprint of WILEY
www.pfeiffer.com

Published by Pfeiffer
An Imprint of Wiley
One Montgomery Street, Suite 1200, San Francisco, CA 94104-4594
www.pfeiffer.com

For additional copies/bulk purchases of this book in the U.S. please contact 800-274-4434.

Pfeiffer books and products are available through most bookstores. To contact Pfeiffer directly call our Customer Care Department within the U.S. at 800-274-4434, outside the U.S. at 317-572-3985, fax 317-572-4002, or visit www.pfeiffer.com.

Pfeiffer publishes in a variety of print and electronic formats and by print-on-demand. Some material included with standard print versions of this book may not be included in e-books or in print-on-demand. If this book refers to media such as a CD or DVD that is not included in the version you purchased, you may download this material at http://booksupport.wiley.com. For more information about Wiley products, visit www.wiley.com.

ISBN: 978-1-118-18272-7

Acquiring Editor: Marisa Kelley   Editor: Rebecca Taff
Director of Development: Kathleen Dolan Davies   Manufacturing Supervisor: Becky Morgan
Development Editor: Janis Chan   Designer: izles design
Production Editor: Dawn Kilgore

Printed in the United States of America

Printing   10 9 8 7 6 5 4 3 2 1

CONTENTS

Introduction .... **PAGE 1**

    Leadership Development Is Self-Development .... **PAGE 1**

    First, Lead Yourself .... **PAGE 2**

    The Best Leaders Are the Best Learners .... **PAGE 2**

    About This Planner .... **PAGE 4**

The Five Practices of Exemplary Leadership .... **PAGE 7**

**Continuing Your Leadership
Development Journey** .... **PAGE 9**

    Overview of the Leadership Development Process .... **PAGE 9**

Review Your Progress .... **PAGE 11**

Refocus Your Developmental Efforts .... **PAGE 13**

    Leadership Behaviors Organized by Practice .... **PAGE 14**

Make a New Plan .... **PAGE 17**

    Leadership Development Activities .... **PAGE 19**

Sample Leadership Development Worksheet..........................PAGE 50

Leadership Development Worksheet...................................PAGE 52

Go Public with Your Plan ....PAGE 55

Continue Your Development ....PAGE 57

Ten Tips for Becoming a Better Leader................PAGE 59

Resources.................................PAGE 67

Further Reading.................................PAGE 69

About the Authors.................................PAGE 77

INTRODUCTION

Leadership Development Is Self-Development

Everything you will ever do as a leader is based on one audacious assumption. It's the assumption that *you matter.*

Before you can lead others, you have to lead yourself and believe that you can have a positive impact on others. You have to believe that your words can inspire and your actions can move others. You have to believe that what you do counts for something. If you don't, you won't even try. Leadership begins with you.

The truth is that you make a difference.

The question is not, "Will I make a difference?" Rather it is, "What difference will I make?"

Leadership is not preordained. It is not a gene, and it is not a trait. There is no hard evidence to support the assertion that leadership is imprinted in the DNA of only some individuals. Leaders reside in every city and every country, in every function and every organization. Leadership knows no racial or religious bounds, no ethnic or cultural borders. It's not a secret code that can only be deciphered by certain people. It has nothing to do with position or status, and everything to do with *behavior*. It is an *observable set of skills and abilities* that are useful whether one is in the executive suite or on the front line, on Wall Street or Main Street, in your own country or on the other side of the world.

FIRST, LEAD YOURSELF

The quest for leadership is first an inner quest to discover who you are. Through self-development comes the confidence needed to lead. Self-confidence is really awareness of and faith in your own powers. These powers become clear and strong only as you work to identify and develop them.

Learning to lead is about discovering what you care about and value. About what inspires you. About what challenges you. About what gives you power and competence. About what encourages you. When you discover these things about yourself, you'll know what it takes to lead those qualities out of others.

Every leader has to learn the fundamentals and the discipline, and to a certain extent there's some period during which you're trying out a lot of new things. It's a necessary stage in your development as a leader. The point is that you have to take what's been acquired and reshape it into your own expression of yourself.

Sometimes liberation is as uncomfortable as intrusion, but in the end when you discover things for yourself you know that what's inside is what you found there and what belongs there. It's not something put inside you by someone else; it's what you discover for yourself.

THE BEST LEADERS ARE THE BEST LEARNERS

After more than thirty years of research, we know that leadership can be learned. It is an observable pattern of practices and behaviors, and a definable set of skills and abilities. Skills can be learned, and when we track the activities of people who participate in leadership development programs, we observe that they improve over time. They become better leaders as long as they engage in activities that help them learn.

But that does not mean that everyone wants to learn to be a leader, and not all those who learn about leadership master it. Why? Because becoming the best requires having a strong desire to excel, a strong belief that new skills and abilities can be learned, and a willing devotion to deliberate practice and continuous learning.

There's no such thing as instant leadership—or instant expertise of any kind. According to the experts on expertise, what truly differentiates the expert performers from the good performers is hours and hours of practice—deliberate practice. The truth is that the best leaders are the best learners. It is only through deliberate practice—focused, planned learning activities designed to improve a specific aspect of performance, usually with a trainer or coach as a guide—and drawing on proven tools such as this Planner and the LPI that you can develop your leadership capacity. That is true whether you want to improve your strengths—the skills you already have—or strengthen your weaker behaviors.

We feel confident that as long as you assume that you can learn to become a better leader than you are now, you can discover your full leadership potential. You've already started by taking the LPI and learning from the feedback you received. Now we invite you to continue on your lifelong learning journey.

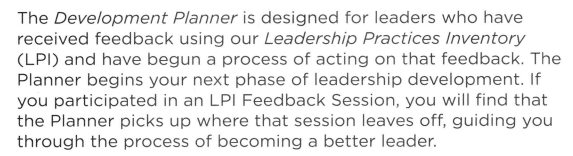

About This Planner

The *Development Planner* is designed for leaders who have received feedback using our *Leadership Practices Inventory* (LPI) and have begun a process of acting on that feedback. The Planner begins your next phase of leadership development. If you participated in an LPI Feedback Session, you will find that the Planner picks up where that session leaves off, guiding you through the process of becoming a better leader.

While you can use the Planner on your own, coaching strengthens the likelihood that you will train and practice. We strongly encourage you to seek out someone who can help you stick with the process, ask you about how you're doing, and give you advice and counsel along the way. If you can't find a coach, however formal or informal the relationship, consider making use of The Leadership Challenge Mobile App, which provides you with opportunities to both set goals and hold yourself accountable for making progress.

Use this Planner as a resource that you can adapt to meet your own needs and come back to time after time. Here are some ways in which you might use it:

- In a workshop in which you more fully explore ways to improve on the behaviors assessed in the LPI.

- In an expert coaching process in which you regularly meet one-on-one with a leadership specialist to see how you are doing and identify new goals.

- In a peer coaching process in which you meet periodically with other leaders who have taken the LPI and are also using the Planner to improve their leadership behaviors.

- In a self-directed leadership development program of your own.

As a result of completing this Planner you will be better able to:

- Develop your own leadership philosophy statements.

- Integrate the best leadership learning practices into your own routines.

- Consciously review your progress toward becoming a better leader.

- Select the kinds of developmental activities that best fit your needs.

- Write a plan for the next steps in your leadership development.

- Apply an easy-to-use process that can be repeated.

Here's what you'll find in the pages that follow:

- A quick review of The Five Practices of Exemplary Leadership®—the fundamentals of leadership on which this Planner is based and which we discuss at length in our book, *The Leadership Challenge: How to Make Extraordinary Things Happen*.

- An overview of the leadership development process you will learn in this Planner.

- Questions to help you review the progress you've made in becoming a better leader since you took the LPI.

- Questions to help you refocus your developmental efforts by identifying your new priorities.

- Questions, suggested development activities, and a worksheet you can use to make your new Leadership Development Plan and go public with your plan.

- Suggestions for continuing your development.

- Ten tips for becoming a better leader drawn from leaders, leadership coaches, and research.

- A list of resources that you will find helpful as you continue on your leadership journey.

Note: This Planner is designed as a workbook, with checkboxes, space to write your responses to questions, and a Leadership Development Worksheet for you to complete. You might want to re-use these pages, so you can find an electronic version here: **www.leadershipchallenge.com/go/lpiworksheet**

THE FIVE PRACTICES OF EXEMPLARY LEADERSHIP

The Five Practices of Exemplary Leadership® and the LPI resulted from an intensive research project to determine the leadership behaviors that are essential to making extraordinary things happen in organizations. That research is what gives credibility to the items on the LPI and the data on the LPI Feedback Report.

Our research clearly indicates that if you do more of the behaviors related to The Five Practices as measured by the LPI, you will get better results in your work, your relationships, and your life. To conduct the research, we collected thousands of "Personal Best" stories—the experiences people recalled when asked to think of a peak leadership experience. Despite differences in individual stories, the Personal-Best Leadership Experiences revealed similar patterns of behavior. The study found that when leaders are at their personal best, they do the following:

MODEL THE WAY

Leaders clarify values by finding their voice and affirming shared values, and they set the example by aligning their actions with the shared values.

INSPIRE A SHARED VISION

Leaders envision the future by imagining exciting and ennobling possibilities, and they enlist others in a common vision by appealing to shared aspirations.

CHALLENGE THE PROCESS

Leaders search for opportunities by seizing the initiative and looking outward for innovative ways to improve, and they experiment and take risks by constantly generating small wins and learning from experience.

ENABLE OTHERS TO ACT

Leaders foster collaboration by building trust and facilitating relationships, and they strengthen others by increasing self-determination and developing competence.

ENCOURAGE THE HEART

Leaders recognize contributions by showing appreciation for individual excellence, and they celebrate values and victories by creating a spirit of community.

Each of The Five Practices of Exemplary Leadership® corresponds with six behaviors from the thirty-item *Leadership Practices Inventory* (LPI). Across continents, The Five Practices have survived the test of time. Although the context may have changed since we began our work more than thirty years ago, the content has remained constant. The fundamental behaviors, actions, and practices of leaders have remained essentially the same since we first began researching and writing about leadership. Much has changed in the world, but there's a whole lot more that's stayed the same. The Planner is designed to facilitate your exploration of the timeless fundamentals that you must master in order to excel as a leader.

For more detailed information about our research, please visit **www.leadershipchallenge.com/go/research.**

CONTINUING YOUR LEADERSHIP DEVELOPMENT JOURNEY

Getting feedback and making development plans is not a one-time-only event. It is a process that the best leaders engage in continuously. You began that process when you analyzed your LPI Feedback Report.

This Planner will help you continue your leadership development journey by creating a robust plan for improvement that you can repeat again and again. The process is based on what research has shown are the planning elements that motivate people to change: Set a goal, make a plan, understand the benefits of changing, and go public with the plan.

Overview of the Leadership Development Process

The process for becoming a better leader includes these steps:

1. Think about where you are now. What are you working on? What's working and what's not? What small wins have you had, and what stands in your way?

2. Go back to your LPI feedback and decide what you would like to work on next. What behaviors do you want to practice frequently? What behaviors do you want to strengthen?

3. Make a plan. Set a goal, determine what you will do to achieve your goal, think about the benefits of achieving it. Then go public with your plan.

4. Obtain feedback and support and reflect on your progress as you work.

5. Set a new goal. When you have achieved your goal, identify new behaviors to work on and develop a new plan.

Here are two important things to keep in mind as you work:

- The best leaders are the best learners. Learning requires self-confidence to honestly examine oneself, self-awareness to seek feedback and suggestions, and self-discipline to engage in new behaviors. Learning always involves mistakes, errors, miscalculations, and the like along the way. Learning happens when you reflect on an experience, can openly talk about what went wrong as well as what went right, and ask, "What can I learn?"

- Getting better as a leader is often about incremental improvements, not huge one-time transformations. It's about what we call "small wins' or "little victories." Extraordinary things aren't done in huge leaps forward; they are done one step at a time, by constantly generating small wins and learning from experience. A small-wins approach fits especially well with the fast and fragmented pace in today's workplace.

REVIEW YOUR PROGRESS

Begin the next leg of your leadership development journey by reviewing the progress you have made since you took the LPI and analyzed your feedback.

■ What actions have you taken?

....

- -

....

- -

■ How is it going? What is working, and what do you still need to work on?

....

- -

....

- -

■ What small wins have you had? What did you learn from them?

....

- -

....

- -

■ What obstacles have you encountered? What might you be able to do about them?

....

....

■ Can you think of any leadership opportunities in your typical day that you might have missed?

....

....

■ Can you identify opportunities for more or better coaching and feedback in this next leg of your journey?

....

....

■ What have you learned about yourself?

....

....

REFOCUS YOUR DEVELOPMENTAL EFFORTS

Now that you've reviewed your progress, take a fresh look at your LPI Feedback Report—the messages your observers sent you and your own self-reflection. Then think about the progress you have made and what you have learned and identify your new priorities.

Note: If you participated in an LPI feedback session, also take another look at your responses to the questions in the LPI Workbook on page 21.

- Now that you've had some time to let the LPI feedback settle in, what observations do you have about your scores?

- What behaviors do you feel comfortable with, yet want to keep practicing?

- What behaviors do you engage in less frequently and want to strengthen?

- On the list of LPI items on the next page, circle the behaviors that are your top priorities at this time—one or two behaviors that you want to keep practicing and one or two behaviors that you want to strengthen. Then move on to page 17, where you will develop a new plan.

Leadership Behaviors Organized by Practice

 MODEL THE WAY

1. I set a personal example of what I expect of others.

6. I spend time and energy making certain that the people I work with adhere to the principles and standards we have agreed on.

11. I follow through on promises and commitments that I make.

16. I ask for feedback on how my actions affect other people's performance.

21. I build consensus around a common set of values for running our organization.

26. I am clear about my philosophy of leadership.

 INSPIRE A SHARED VISION

2. I talk about future trends that will influence how our work gets done.

7. I describe a compelling image of what our future could be like.

12. I appeal to others to share an exciting dream of the future.

17. I show others how their long-term interests can be realized by enlisting in a common vision.

22. I paint the "big picture" of what we aspire to accomplish.

27. I speak with genuine conviction about the higher meaning and purpose of our work.

CHALLENGE THE PROCESS

3. I seek out challenging opportunities that test my own skills and abilities.

8. I challenge people to try out new and innovative ways to do their work.

13. I search outside the formal boundaries of my organization for innovative ways to improve what we do.

18. I ask "What can we learn?" when things don't go as expected.

23. I make certain that we set achievable goals, make concrete plans, and establish measurable milestones for the projects and programs that we work on.

28. I experiment and take risks, even when there is a chance of failure.

ENABLE OTHERS TO ACT

4. I develop cooperative relationships among the people I work with.

9. I actively listen to diverse points of view.

14. I treat others with dignity and respect.

19. I support the decisions that people make on their own.

24. I give people a great deal of freedom and choice in deciding how to do their work.

29. I ensure that people grow in their jobs by learning new skills and developing themselves.

ENCOURAGE THE HEART

5. I praise people for a job well done.

10. I make it a point to let people know about my confidence in their abilities.

15. I make sure that people are creatively rewarded for their contributions to the success of our projects.

20. I publicly recognize people who exemplify commitment to shared values.

25. I find ways to celebrate accomplishments.

30. I give the members of the team lots of appreciation and support for their contributions.

MAKE A NEW PLAN

Now that you have identified your new priorities, you are ready to set your new goal, determine what actions you will take to achieve it and what the benefits of achieving it are likely to be, and identify people who can give you advice, support, and feedback as you work.

Do the following:

1. Read the suggested developmental actions for practicing or improving each of the LPI behaviors on pages 19 to 48. Circle any suggestions that seem particularly relevant to your current priorities and situation.

2. Take a look at the sample Leadership Development Worksheet on pages 50 and 51.

3. Using the sample as a guide, complete the blank worksheet on pages 52 and 53.

Leadership Development Activities

MODEL THE WAY

LPI Statement

1. I set a personal example of what is expected.

Development Activities

- Write down the top ten expectations for your work group. Score yourself on a scale of 1 to 5 on how well you are doing on each expectation (1 = not at all; 2 = occasionally; 3 = sometimes; 4 = often; 5 = very frequently). Then reflect on what actions you can take to lead in a different way.
- Think about one of your staff's expectations of you as a leader. How have you demonstrated this expectation to your staff?
- Schedule time to clearly outline what you expect of others. Then objectively review how you live up to those same expectations.
- Show up unannounced and take over a task from one of your team members—something that might not be the most pleasant (yet necessary) part of the person's job.
- Create a blog that publishes both your promises and your progress toward meeting these commitments. Invite your team members or constituents to comment and participate in the ongoing posts.
- _____
- _____

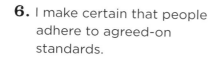

6. I make certain that people adhere to agreed-on standards.

■ Write down the top five standards for your work group and score your team on a scale of 1 to 5 on how well they are doing on each expectation (1 = not at all; 2 = occasionally; 3 = sometimes; 4 = often; 5 = very frequently). Reflect on what feedback and coaching you can provide to team members about when they have succeeded at meeting the standards and when they may have fallen short.

■ List the standards that you think are the most important and share them with your team.

■ Invite dialogue among the team to clarify everyone's understanding of the standards and principles, and discuss how they drive the team's decisions and actions.

■ Schedule a recurring time each week to walk around your workspace and personally check in with your colleagues. When you discover an example of someone living up to the team's or organization's standards, be sure to acknowledge the person and praise his or her effort.

■ Create an audio podcast as a forum to broadcast the team's values and to demonstrate how their actions have aligned with these values.

■ _____

■ _____

11. I follow through on the promises and commitments that I make.

- Write down all your commitments and promises, especially those you make "in the hallway." Monitor your behaviors and actions and track how often you follow through. Conduct this self-audit on a regular basis to ensure continued improvement.

- Often people who have a low score on this commitment have a habit of saying "yes" to everything out of a desire to exceed the expectations of internal and external customers. To develop in this area, look at your current "to do" list and ask yourself the following questions:

  - What is the priority for each task?
  - How many of the tasks are "overdue."
  - Which of the tasks should I have delegated or not taken on? Why? What can I be doing differently right now or could I do differently next time?

- To ensure you will have time to do what you say you will do, go through your calendar and decline some meetings that there is no reason for you to attend.

- _____

- _____

16. I ask for feedback on how my actions affect people's performance.

- At the end of each one-on-one meeting with your direct reports, ask: "What do you need from me to perform your job better? What could I do differently as a leader to help you be more successful?" If you do not have direct reports, ask your teammates, "What could I do differently as a teammate to be a better leader?"
- Select your most recent meeting, client interaction, or project and ask someone else his/her thoughts about the impact of something you did and how you might do this even better in the future.
- Once a month, take a team member out for coffee or lunch. Ask him or her what you are doing that helps his or her work, and what you are doing that hinders that work.
- Set up a Twitter account for an appropriate project or initiative. Ask your team members or constituents to report developments, and react to ideas and suggestions.

- _____

- _____

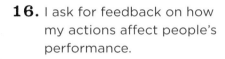

21. I build consensus around the organization's values.

- Make a list of values in your organization. Include the company values and the operating values of your team (the mutually understood norms for how you work together) and ensure that this list is visible to your team. Conduct a team meeting to elicit the team's understanding of its operating values.

- Link the organization's values to the work and behaviors of the team. Ask others to note when the team lives out the values and when they don't. Given this feedback, take action accordingly.

- Ask team members to make lists of their top five personal values. Then ask them how their personal values align with the common set of team or organizational values.

- Ask a team member or constituent to recount how a shared value was recently demonstrated and publish it as an audio podcast. For example, a two- to three-minute "going the extra mile" for a customer story might be highly effective.

- _____

- _____

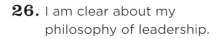

26. I am clear about my
philosophy of leadership.

- Review your personal values and write down
  what you believe about what is important for
  your leadership in one paragraph that begins
  with "I believe . . ."

- On an index card, write down one point of
  your leadership philosophy. At the end of the
  week, write on the back of the card how you
  lived this out.

- Write a short personal leadership mission
  statement and hang it in clear sight.

- Schedule a time to record yourself sharing
  your philosophy of leadership and listen to it
  again to assure it is clear and concise.

- Create a wiki that outlines what you believe
  are the shared values of your team or
  constituents. Have members of your team or
  organization create, amend, or improve the
  published content. Use the feedback to test
  your own notions of leadership clarity.

- _____

- _____

INSPIRE A SHARED VISION

LPI Statement

2. I talk about future trends that will influence how our work gets done.

Development Activities

- Research industry publications, blogs, websites, etc., and find one trend that you see in your industry. Ask yourself: "How will this affect our industry? Our company? My team? What can we do to be prepared/out in front of the change?" Discuss this with the team and talk about potential changes.

- Ask another team member to engage in the same research process for a future meeting. Repeat, rotating the responsibility throughout the team.

- Schedule a time to talk with a member of your technology team. Interview him or her about the exciting new technologies that are on the horizon.

- Spend some time on **www.ted.com** and choose a particularly inspiring video to support a trends discussion with your team.

- _____

- _____

7. I describe a compelling image of what our future could be like.

- Write down four reasons why you are excited about the future. Think about how you can make these four reasons exciting to others.

- Practice creating imagery for yourself by picking your ideal vacation spot, imagining that money and time are plentiful. Visualize the best future vacation in this spot—not what you've done in the past, but what you could do with all the money and time in the world. What would it look like? What would you do? Where would you stay? Write down the details of your first day on that vacation, including the images and the senses (what you see, hear, smell, taste). Reflect on how you would tell others about it. Then use your imagination to do the same for a current project. How would you tell others about it?

- Ask a colleague to listen to your description of your compelling image of the future; then ask that person to share what he or she heard you say in his or her own words so you can evaluate the effectiveness of sharing the message. Ask for constructive feedback.

- Create a blog and post the latest version of your vision statement. Invite members of your team or organization to comment and react to the post.

- _____

- _____

12. I appeal to others to share an exciting dream of the future.

- Link the team's daily activities to the bigger picture so that people can see themselves in the vision.

- List your current constituents and their personal values. If you do not know, make a guess based on your experience with each individual, or better yet, ask the person. As you reflect on the future state of any project or process, think of what may appeal to each constituent as you communicate the group's shared vision.

- Listen to Martin Luther King's "I have a dream" speech. Note three to five techniques he uses to communicate his vision. Then write a clear, concise statement of your vision of the future incorporating some of the techniques he used and practice communicating your vision to your constituents.

- Set up a Twitter account and encourage team or constituent participation. You might offer the first tweet describing your own vision as a way to start the conversation.

- _____

- _____

17. I show others how their long-term interests can be realized by enlisting in a common vision.

■ Connect the interest of others to the work that they do, and find opportunities for them to explore their interests.

■ Often individuals are wondering, "WIIFM?" ("What's in it for me?"). Communicate this as well as "WIIFU?" ("What's in it for us?") as you discuss key initiatives with your team.

■ Ask team members to describe what they see as the vision for the team and compare it to the shared vision you have articulated. Follow up by asking what role each team member sees in supporting the vision. Take whatever actions are needed to ensure that everyone is on the same page.

■ Create a wiki for your team or constituents. Post a team or organization vision and offer suggestions on how the vision serves everyone's long-term interests.

■ _____

■ _____

18. I paint the "big picture" of what we aspire to accomplish.

- Create a collage where all the team members put up a picture or pictures of what they aspire to. Draw from these themes to create a message.

- When talking about key initiatives, projects, etc., connect the work of your team members with the goals of the organization by discussing the ways in which the initiatives and projects are connected to key organizational goals and strategies.

- During a team meeting, hand out paper and markers. Ask team members to draw what they "see" in the big picture, based on what you've described.

- When speaking about what you and your colleagues are doing today, be sure to indicate how this is taking all of you to some place in the future.

- Think of the "big picture" as analogous to the image on the box top of a jigsaw puzzle. Everyone has a "piece of the puzzle" that contributes to creating the whole. Tell your team members what that larger image is and how their pieces contribute to creating it.

- _____

- _____

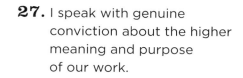

27. I speak with genuine conviction about the higher meaning and purpose of our work.

- Tell a good story about what the work is really doing: saving lives, making life easier, etc.
- Verbally recognize instances of the company's mission, vision, or values being brought to life through actions of team members.
- Ask yourself one of the following questions. After your initial answer, ask "Why is that important to me?" Respond and ask, "Why" again. Repeat five times to gain clarity about your passion. Here are some additional questions to reflect on:
  - What do you stand for? Why?
  - What do you believe in? Why?
  - What are you discontented about? Why?
  - What brings you suffering? Why?
  - What makes you weep and wail? Why?
  - What makes you jump for joy? Why?
  - What are you passionate about? Why?
  - What keeps you awake at night? Why?
  - What's grabbed hold and won't let go? Why?
  - What do you want for your life? Why?
  - Just what is it that you really care about? Why?
- Find ways to share each person's response to these questions with all other team members. They could do it in a blog, a LinkedIn group, a series of tweets, podcasts, or in a meeting. The point is for people to talk about the higher meaning and purpose of their work.
- Ask a member of your team or another constituent to share his or her convictions about work.
- _____
- _____

CHALLENGE THE PROCESS

LPI Statement

3. I seek out challenging opportunities that test my own skills and abilities.

Development Activities

- Identify one skill that you need to expand or test. What can you do within thirty days to test this skill?
- Reflect on an area of your leadership that you would like to improve and seek out a project that will help you develop that area.
- Choose a task, role, or department within your organization that you would like to learn more about. Then find an expert in that choice and ask that person to teach you everything he or she knows.
- Sign up for a class or tackle a do-it-yourself project and have fun in the process of learning something new without being focused on perfection.
- Seek out a work assignment that stretches you and requires you to learn new things.

- _____

- _____

8. I challenge people to try out new and innovative ways to do their work.

- Ask your team to give you at least three different ways to solve a problem.
- Ask yourself what processes may need to change based on client or partner feedback. Challenge those you work with to come up with a brief outline of five new ways to do that process. Have them discuss "Why won't that one work?" and "Why will that one work?"
- Create a blog and give it a name such as New Thinking Journal or the Status Quo Challenge. As you discover new, innovative, or more productive ways of doing things, post the most appropriate findings and encourage others to comment or post their own ideas.
- Where can you give people on your team an opportunity to do something that they have never done before?
- Once a week at a meeting, in an email, in a blog, or one-on-one ask each of your team members this question: "What have you done in the last week to improve so that you are more effective this week than you were a week ago?" Make sure to ask this question regularly.

- _____

- _____

13. I search outside the formal boundaries of my organization for innovative ways to improve.

■ Take your team on at least one field trip to a store, museum, or mall with the intent of looking for what people are doing that you might use to help improve processes or experiences.

■ Ask team members to read a book, watch a movie, or interview people from other industries about how they achieve excellence, provide customer service, ensure their products are of high quality, educate their team, etc., and discuss what they learned with the team.

■ Begin looking at the world with wonder, asking yourself when you see things, "I wonder where that idea came from?" Start to apply your answers to your own work.

■ Schedule regular appointments with a successful leader at a company or organization outside your industry or sector. Learn more about the leader's philosophy, practices, behaviors, and how he or she applies leadership to running a successful organization.

■ Seek others in your own industry who are doing things differently and achieving positive results.

■ Ask your team members, "What organization, regardless of industry, is best at 'X' (and 'X' can be anything you want—service, product development, training, marketing, etc.)?" Then ask, "What would that company do if they were going about 'X'?"

■ _____

■ _____

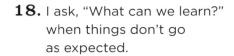

18. I ask, "What can we learn?" when things don't go as expected.

■ Do a project debriefing for both those that are successful and those that had a few hiccups along the way. Ask, "What do we need to move forward? What have we learned that made us better or that needs improvement?"

■ Ask "What have we learned?" at the end of every meeting and encourage colleagues and team members to provide feedback and ideas more frequently.

■ Research "Appreciative Inquiry" and apply its steps to the next project that doesn't achieve the desired outcomes.

■ Create a wiki to build a community of users who support the idea of learning from mistakes.

■ _____

■ _____

23. I make certain that we set achievable goals, make concrete plans, and establish measurable milestones for the projects and programs we work on.

- Make goals, plans, and milestones visible to all.
- Find a creative way to track progress and involve others with the tracking.
- As a team, review the project and ask the team to develop the needed goals, plans, and milestones needed to achieve completion.
- Create a wiki for a complex project and post the project plan.
- Invite members of the project team or group to think creatively and break the process down into smaller, achievable steps.
- Each day publicly acknowledge the progress that has been made. If there were setbacks, tell people not to be discouraged and that tomorrow we will all take another step forward.

- _____

- _____

28. I experiment and take risks, even when there is a chance of failure.

■ Schedule conversations with key people and discuss how taking bigger risks will help the organization reach its goals faster.

■ When you take a risk, share the risk and your learning with others. Share both successful and unsuccessful risks.

■ Reflect on a "big" risk that you've not been willing to take because it was daunting. Determine what you could do if you were to take "half" the risk—and do that!

■ Challenge yourself to take a class, tackle a do-it-yourself project, or another way to "walk on the edge of your comfort zone."

■ Enlist members to send tweets that encourage innovative thinking and risk taking on current or future projects.

■ Instead of thinking about the risk, think about the potential gains (which might very well outweigh any risk) or make it possible to say "We can't *not* take the risk to do this."

■ _____

■ _____

LPI Statement

4. I develop cooperative relationships among the people I work with.

Development Activities

- Identify a person on your team you need to find out more about and take a 15-minute break with him or her.

- Identify two key relationships that you should be paying more attention to. Invite those individuals to coffee or lunch to discuss what goals you are each working on and how you can help each other achieve those goals—even if they appear to be competing.

- Build relationships with other departments or teams by having a "take turns" lunch. One month, your department makes or buys lunch for the other department, and the next month it's the other department's turn.

- Pick a recently completed project or initiative in which cooperation played a key role in its success. Ask two or more team members to participate. Publish the audio podcast and discuss it at your next team or constituent meeting.

- _____

- _____

9. I actively listen to diverse points of view.

- Take a few minutes in a regularly scheduled project meeting for everyone to share a new idea that pertains to the project.

- Practice intentional listening by paraphrasing back to people what you heard.

- When faced with a perspective or counter-point with which you don't immediately agree, resist the temptation to challenge the other person. Instead, ask, "How can you help me learn more about your perspective?"

- Create a new blog or use an existing account and invite your team members or constituents to comment on a project or initiative. For example, you might describe a project with several scenarios being considered. Ask for the input of others and show your respect and trust through your comments.

- As you listen to folks, consider asking them what they would view as the other side of their argument. Listen to that as well.

- When you are seeking new and innovative ideas, put together a team of people from different disciplines to brainstorm ideas.

- _____

- _____

14. I treat others with dignity and respect.

- Make it a point to address people by name.
- With your team, brainstorm what dignity and respect "look like." Make sure that these behaviors are well-articulated and understood by everyone on the team.
- Use Twitter to invite others to comment on what they feel shows trust or respect from a leader.
- Find out more about the people you work with, especially about their interests and talents outside of the workplace. Get to know them as "whole" people.

- _____

- _____

19. I support the decisions that people make on their own.

- Verbally affirm your support when other people make decisions.

- Challenge yourself to NOT correct your constituents' work/ideas/etc. automatically. Instead, ask for context around ideas that you may be wary of, thus creating an environment in which you ask for ideas rather than dictate how something must be done.

- Withholding judgment, allow team members the autonomy to make their own decisions, given the appropriate situations with a clear understanding of the parameters. Once the decision is made, support the follow-through, and course-correct with the team member as needed.

- Create a wiki and give your team or constituents free reign to design the workflow for a new project or process. Take the opportunity to coach and support their decisions.

- _____

- _____

24. I give people a great deal of freedom and choice in deciding how to do their work.

- List some of the special skills that your team members or direct reports have. Now identify why they are capable of making great decisions.
- Set clear expectations of what needs to be done and let people figure out how to achieve them.
- Identify something that you can delegate to a constituent and ask the person how he or she could do it differently or better in order to obtain the same or better results.
- Initiate or assign projects based on the end in mind. Describe to team members what the end or final outcomes will look like, and allow them to choose the ways to get there.
- Find ways to give your "power" away to other people; learn to delegate effectively, and more often.

- _____

- _____

29. I ensure that people grow in their jobs.

- Get to know people and what they do; then give them opportunities to grow to the next step with your support. Make this a part of their development plans.

- Compare each of your constituent's level of competence to the challenges he or she faces. Ask yourself, "Does this person have the skills to meet the challenges?" If not, what kind of training and development does he or she need?

- Allow team members to choose cross-training experiences in other areas of the organization in which they can apply their strengths while learning something new.

- Create a **ning.com** social network on the topic of learning. Give the social network an appropriate name such as the Learning Group or other name that describes the purpose. Invite team members and constituents to sign up and participate in the discussion about learning needs. The network can also provide on-the-spot informal learning for some members.

- _____

- _____

ENCOURAGE THE HEART

LPI Statement

5. I praise people for a job well done.

Development Activities

- Make a practice of sending at least one handwritten thank-you note a day to someone you've caught doing something right. Don't think you can do this? We know a CEO who wrote fifty a day.
- Schedule a 15-minute appointment on your calendar to call someone who is helping you with a project and thank him or her for the great job he or she is doing.
- When praising people, make sure you are sharing not only what they did, but also why it was important and the impact that it had on others.
- For one week, pay closer attention to how frequently you give praise. Keep an audit of how many times you praise people, for what, and how.
- When you see high performance in action or extraordinary effort, use Twitter to send the news to the connected social network.
- _____
- _____

10. I make it a point to let people know about my confidence in their abilities.

- ▨ Take the time to notice what people are good at and tell them. Be specific.

- ▨ Talk to team members about areas where they'd like to stretch and grow, and give them assignments that stretch their skill and challenge them, with the right amount of support (authority and responsibility).

- ▨ Make it a point to talk about your constituents' strengths in meetings with your colleagues or superiors.

- ▨ Create a new wiki and post recent achievements or celebrate well-executed projects. Using this format lets others participate in defining the significance and also builds a community of shared values.

- ▨ In your regular staff meetings, be sure to include a time to point out those who have done the right thing—learned a new skill, tackled a problem, dealt effectively with a difficult client, and the like.

- ▨ _____

- ▨ _____

15. I make sure that people are creatively rewarded for their contributions to the success of our projects.

- Read a book on rewarding people and find one idea that you can implement.
- Write down something that each of your constituents personally enjoys. Use this list as a starting point for determining how you might reward them for their contributions and/or create a simple metaphor to incorporate into your recognition for each person.
- Come up with a fun way to recognize creativity, like a cool t-shirt or jacket that others will recognize when they see it. It does not necessarily need to be expensive; it just needs to stand out.
- Create an ETH award bucket or basket with toys, awards, and trinkets. Encourage team members to give awards to their peers as on-the-spot recognition, with an explanation of what behavior is being rewarded and why it makes a difference to the overall success of the team.
- Use Twitter to invite team members or constituents to share something funny or interesting that will make other team members or constituents smile. Post a funny picture; describe a humorous incident that happened.
- Take a moment to ask each of your direct reports, even colleagues, how they would like you to let them know that you believe they have done a good job. Then do these things, as appropriate.

- _____

- _____

20. I publicly recognize people who exemplify commitment to shared values.

- Choose a shared value and be watchful of how this value comes to life in the organization. Talk about what you see.

- Make a list of values in your organization, including company values and operating values of your team (What are the understood values for how you work together?) and ensure that these are visible to your team and create encouragements/rewards for those who exemplify those values.

- When you see it, say it. Praise people for a job well done. Be specific and let their peers hear you praise them. This will reinforce and spread desired behaviors.

- Create a way for team members to recognize each other for contributions. It could be as simple as a printable card that says someone is a rock star or a big poster in the break room.

- Create a new **ning.com** network specifically for celebrating individual contributions and invite your constituents to post stories, photos, or videos that help tell the story of the contribution.

- _____

- _____

25. I find ways to celebrate our accomplishments.

- Define celebrations as part of the project plan, not afterward. When planning a project, include celebrations at the milestones so that those around you feel appreciated for their work.

- Send a thank-you note not only to team member(s) involved in the accomplishment but also to their family members to thank them for their support.

- If your organization has an internal newsletter, website, or portal, create a special section for highlighting select people for their accomplishments.

- Create a "Great Work!" or "Go Team" blog and invite your team members or constituents to participate with you as excellent work is celebrated.

- You don't have to do this all by yourself. Consult with others on your team about how to best celebrate milestones along the way.

- _____

- _____

30. I give members of the team lots of appreciation and support for their contributions.

- Implement a program to recognize people for high performance. Make it an ongoing program that allows for peer-to-peer recognition, too.
- Before a meeting, think about why you should appreciate the team. Then say it.
- At the end of each day, sincerely thank those who work with you for what they have done that day.
- Set the example by encouraging team members to offer encouragement to each other.
- Be generous when it comes to saying "thank you" around your workplace. Don't take anyone for granted.
- Be sure to "brag" about your team members to people outside of your organization. Even if your team members aren't there, they're likely to hear about it from others.

- _____

- _____

Sample Leadership Development Worksheet

TODAY'S DATE: May 1, 2013

LEADERSHIP DEVELOPMENT PERIOD: May 2–22, 2013

MY TWO TOP PRIORITIES FOR THIS PERIOD: Write a compelling vision statement and present it to my team

- A LEADERSHIP BEHAVIOR TO KEEP PRACTICING: Model the Way: Continue asking for feedback from team members on how my actions affect their performance

- A LEADERSHIP BEHAVIOR TO STRENGTHEN: Inspire a Shared Vision: Describe a compelling image of the future and enlist team members in that common vision

MY GOALS (WHAT I WANT TO ACHIEVE): Write and present a compelling vision of the future that my team shares

THE BENEFITS OF ACHIEVING THESE GOALS: We will be energized and enthusiastic about working together toward our common goal; we will be more productive; we will be better able to achieve our team's mission.

MY MEASURE OF SUCCESS (HOW I WILL KNOW WHEN I HAVE REACHED MY GOALS): Team members give me feedback that lets me know they understand and share my vision.

ACTIONS I WILL TAKE TO ACHIEVE MY GOALS

- ACTION: Write a 5 to 7 minute vision statement

- DATE BY WHICH I WILL TAKE THIS ACTION: May 8

- ACTION: Ask for feedback on my draft vision statement from Luis, who does this better than anyone I know, revise it, ask him to review the revised draft, and make any additional changes that might be needed

- DATE BY WHICH I WILL TAKE THIS ACTION: May 15

- ACTION: Present my vision statement to my team, ask for their feedback, revise it again, and present the revised statement to the team

- DATE BY WHICH I WILL TAKE THIS ACTION: May 22

PEOPLE WHO WILL GIVE ME FEEDBACK: Luis and my team members

PEOPLE WHO WILL PROVIDE SUPPORT: My manager, Teri, and my team members

Leadership Development Worksheet

TODAY'S DATE:

LEADERSHIP DEVELOPMENT PERIOD:

MY TWO TOP PRIORITIES FOR THIS PERIOD:

- A LEADERSHIP BEHAVIOR TO KEEP PRACTICING:

- A LEADERSHIP BEHAVIOR TO STRENGTHEN:

MY GOALS (WHAT I WANT TO ACHIEVE):

THE BENEFITS OF ACHIEVING THESE GOALS:

MY MEASURE OF SUCCESS (HOW I WILL KNOW WHEN I HAVE REACHED MY GOALS):

ACTIONS I WILL TAKE TO ACHIEVE MY GOALS

■ ACTION:

■ DATE BY WHICH I WILL TAKE THIS ACTION:

■ ACTION:

■ DATE BY WHICH I WILL TAKE THIS ACTION:

■ ACTION:

■ DATE BY WHICH I WILL TAKE THIS ACTION:

PEOPLE WHO WILL GIVE ME FEEDBACK:

PEOPLE WHO WILL PROVIDE SUPPORT:

GO PUBLIC WITH YOUR PLAN

Research has shown that people are more likely to honor their commitments when they share them with others. Telling at least one other person what you intend to do is a way to help ensure that you'll follow through. Tell your manager, your coach, or a close colleague what actions you intend to take and when you will take them. Make an agreement to meet with that person at a certain time to review your progress.

Share the following with the person or people you choose:

- Your top priorities and your reasons for choosing them

- Your goals, the benefits of achieving those goals, the actions you will take for achieving goals, and your timetable

- The people who will provide feedback and support as you work toward your goals

CONTINUE YOUR DEVELOPMENT

Those who are the very best at anything are that way because they had a strong desire to excel, a belief that new skills and abilities can be learned, and a willing devotion to deliberate practice and continuous learning. Of course, change does not happen overnight. The process of reviewing your progress and making new development plans is not a one-time-only event. Real change begins when you turn your workplace into a practice field for leadership.

EVERY DAY, ASK, "HOW AM I DOING?"

An important part of any development process is stepping back and asking, "How am I doing? What did I do today to practice my leadership behaviors? What happened? What leadership opportunities might I have missed?" It's a good idea to ask those questions every day, even when you are very busy, and jot down your observations in a journal or a daily planner. It only takes a few minutes, and you will have those written observations to refer to when you're ready for a more comprehensive review.

SEEK FEEDBACK

Let the people you work with—your direct reports, your manager, and your other constituents—know what you are working on and seek their feedback on an ongoing basis. Make notes in your journal or planner so you can refer to that feedback when you need to adjust your development plan or are ready to develop a new plan. After all, isn't it in their best interests for you to be the best leader you can be?

REGULARLY REVIEW YOUR PROGRESS

At first, look at your Leadership Development Worksheet each day in order to track your progress toward achieving your goals. After you've been practicing for a while, checking progress once a week might work for you.

Just as in any improvement activity, frequent and regular feedback is critical. Make sure you keep asking yourself these kinds of questions: "What's working, and what's not?" "What is getting in my way, and what can I do about it?" "Do I need to make any adjustments to my development plan?" (If you do need to make changes, than make them and continue moving forward!)

MAKE NEW PLANS

When you have achieved your goals, follow the process in this Planner to make a new plan. Think about what you have learned. Take another look at your LPI feedback and select two to four new behaviors to work on. Then complete a new Leadership Development Worksheet with your new goals and go public with your plan. Repeat the process again and again as you improve in certain behaviors and identify other areas in which you can do better.

RETAKE THE LPI

The LPI is a snapshot that shows how you are doing at the time the shutter was clicked. But you didn't take the LPI so you could stay the same. We suggest that you repeat the LPI at least once a year, and preferably every six to nine months, especially if you change jobs or start to work with new constituents. Repeating the LPI provides you with the detailed, structured feedback you need to continue on your journey of becoming the best leader you can be.

TEN TIPS FOR BECOMING A BETTER LEADER

We asked a number of leaders and leadership coaches to share with us their best learning practices for becoming a better leader. We combined their observations with our own and others' research and synthesized these lessons into the following top ten tips. Use them as you review your progress and continue your leadership development efforts.

TIP 1. BE SELF-AWARE

There's solid evidence that the best leaders are highly attuned to what's going on inside of them as they are leading. They're very self-aware. They're also quite aware of the impact they're having on others. In fact, self-awareness may be the most crucial learning skill of all.

Think about it this way. Let's say you begin to hear an odd sound every time you start your car. You ignore it, and pretty soon you don't even notice it any more. You just keep on driving. Then one day your car won't start at all. The mechanic tells you that it would have been a simple, inexpensive problem to fix if you had paid attention when it first started, but because you ignored it for so long, it's going to cost a bundle.

The same is true in leading. Self-awareness helps you receive clues about what's going on inside you and in your environment. Your emotions are messages. They're trying to teach you something. Don't be afraid of them, and don't become self-conscious about them. Just listen and learn. Take time to reflect on your experiences. Keep a journal of some kind, or record your thoughts and feelings on tape. As you go through your developmental experiences, look within yourself and pay attention to how you're feeling.

TIP 2. MANAGE YOUR EMOTIONS

While the best leaders are self-aware, they are careful not to let their feelings manage them. Instead, they manage their feelings.

Self-control is important. Let's say you become aware that you become angry when people are unprepared for a meeting. One way to respond would be to yell at them and put them down in front of the group. But would that be the best way to handle the situation for the sake of your credibility and your relationship with your constituents? No, it would not.

The same is true in learning. There will be times when you become frustrated and when you become upset at the feedback that you receive. You could go out and break something or yell at someone, but that won't help your learning or your relationships. So manage your emotions. Be aware of them, but don't let them rule your behavior. And if you sense that you need help managing those emotions, seek it.

TIP 3. SEEK FEEDBACK

One of the reasons the best leaders are highly self-aware is that they ask for feedback from others. In fact, the best leaders ask for feedback not only about what they're doing well, but about what they're not doing well. They want to know the negative as well as the positive.

Now you can understand why being able to manage your emotions is so important. Who in his right mind is going to give you negative feedback if he or she knows you're going to get angry? But if people know you genuinely want the feedback, that you'll thank them for it, and that you'll do something with the feedback they give you, then you'll benefit, and so will they. The more specific you can be with your request, the more likely that others will have something to share with you.

When people are learning, others tend to be very forgiving. So tell your constituents what you're trying to do and that you want their honest feedback. Afterward, ask, "How'd I do?" Have a conversation. Then say thanks.

TIP 4. TAKE THE INITIATIVE

Our research is very clear on this point: The best leaders are proactive. They don't wait for someone else to tell them what to do. They take the initiative to find and solve problems and to meet and create challenges. The same is true in learning.

The best leaders don't wait to be told by a manager or by someone in human resources that they need to change their behavior. Instead, they take charge of their own learning. Because they're self-aware and they seek feedback, they know their strengths and areas for improvement and they know what needs to be done. They seek the developmental opportunities they need. If the resources aren't available from the organization, they find a way to gain the experience, example, or education some other way.

It's your learning. It's your career. It's your life. Take charge of it.

TIP 5. ENGAGE A COACH

The top athletes, the top musicians, and the top performing artists all have coaches. Leadership is also a performing art, and the best leaders also have coaches. The coach might be someone from inside or outside of the organization. This person might be a peer, a manager, a trainer, or someone with specific expertise in what you are trying to learn. Coaches can play a number of roles. The most obvious is to watch you perform, give you feedback, and offer suggestions for improvement. But effective coaches can also be a very valuable source of social support, which is essential to resilience and persistence. Support is especially important when people are being asked to change their behavior. When you return to work after training, your initial enthusiasm can be quickly crushed if there is no one around to offer words of encouragement. Every leader needs someone to lean on from time to time. Your coach should be able to offer you not only advice but also attention and caring. The best coaches are good listeners. In fact, they watch and listen about twice as much as they teach and tell.

We've found in our research on coaching that the factor most related to coaching effectiveness is the quality of the relationship between performer and coach. And of all the items used to measure coaching behavior, the one most linked to success is: "This person embodies character qualities and values that I admire." (There's that credibility factor again.)

TIP 6. SET GOALS AND MAKE A PLAN

Exemplary leaders make sure that the work they do to develop themselves is not pointless ambling but purposeful action. Too often people participate in training and development without any clear goals in mind. They never ask themselves: "Why am I here?" "What do I want to get out of this learning experience?" People who attend training programs with a clear sense of what they want to accomplish are much more likely to apply what they learn than those who do not have clear goals. Leadership development has a purpose, and that purpose should be clear to everyone.

Set high expectations for yourself and for your constituents. Adults in the workplace and children in school tend to perform to the level of expectations. The leaders who are the most successful at bringing out the best in others set achievable stretch goals—that is, they set goals that are high, but not so far out of reach that people give up even before they start because they think, "I can never do that." Leaders who succeed in getting high performance also display confidence in other people's abilities to perform. The research is crystal-clear: Leaders who say, "I know you can do it" achieve better results. And leaders who bring out the best in others also believe in their own abilities to coach and train. You have to have confidence in yourself as well as confidence in others to be a good coach. These same principles apply to learning.

It's important to make your goals public. You are more likely to work harder to improve if you tell other people what you're trying to accomplish rather than keeping it to yourself. There is always less commitment when goals are kept private.

Once you've set your goals, make a plan. Figure out the steps from where you are to where you want to be. There may be several options available, just as there are several routes you could take to travel across the country—you just need to pick the one that best suits your needs.

In setting your goals and making your plans, focus on a few things at a time. You may have a strong desire to improve in three of The Five Practices and in ten of the thirty behaviors. That's terrific, but don't attempt to do everything at once. The fact is that

most improvements are incremental. Take it one step at a time. There are no such things as "conversions" to great leadership.

TIP 7. PRACTICE, PRACTICE, PRACTICE

People who practice more often are more likely to become experts at what they do. To be the best you can be, you must not only apply what you learn on the playing field, but you must also hone your skills on the practice field. We know this is true in the performing arts and in sports, but somehow people do not always apply the same idea to leadership. Professional leaders take practice seriously. The practice may be role playing a negotiation, rehearsing a speech, or a one-on-one dialogue with a coach. Whatever it is, practice is essential to learning.

Practice fields also offer the opportunity to try out unfamiliar methods, behaviors, and tools in a safer environment than on-the-job situations. You are more likely to take risks when you feel safe than when you feel highly vulnerable. Since the stakes are higher on the job than on the practice field, give yourself the chance to run some plays in practice before rushing into the game.

You can also treat every experience as a learning experience, even when it's for real. Whether you consider the experience a raving success or a miserable failure, step back and ask yourself and those involved, "What went well? What went poorly?" "What did I do well? What did I do poorly?" "What could we improve?" The best leaders are the best learners, and learning can occur any time, anywhere. Take advantage of that fact.

TIP 8. MEASURE PROGRESS

People need to know whether they're making progress or marking time. Goals help to serve that function, but goals alone are not enough. It's not enough to know that you want to make it to the summit. You also need to know whether you're still climbing—or whether you're sliding downhill.

Measuring progress is crucial to improvement, no matter what the activity. Whether it's strengthening endurance, shedding pounds, increasing sales, or becoming a better leader, knowing how well you've done in terms of the goals you've set is crucial to motivation and achievement. Setting goals without feedback is actually no better in improving performance than setting no goals at all. It's the two together that propel performance forward.

Exemplary leaders and exemplary learners create a system that enables them to monitor and measure progress on a regular basis. The best measurement systems are ones that are visible and instant—like the speedometer on your dashboard or the watch on your wrist. The best measurement systems are also ones that you can check yourself, without having to wait for someone else to tell you. For instance, you can count how many thank-you notes you send out by keeping a log.

A self-monitoring system can include asking for feedback. Others may need to give you the information about how you're doing, but you're in charge of the asking. Another way to monitor your progress is to repeat the administration of the *Leadership Practices Inventory* at least once a year, and preferably every six to nine months.

TIP 9. REWARD YOURSELF

If new behavior is not rewarded, that behavior will be quickly forgotten. Even worse, when you say you want new behavior but actually reward the old behavior, people quickly conclude that you are not serious about the new behavior. For example, let's say you want to create a greater sense of teamwork among your sales force, but instead of setting up a new incentive system that rewards teamwork, you continue to reward people solely on the basis of who sells the most. It's likely that your salespeople will continue the behavior that is rewarded.

Connect your performance to rewards. It's nice when others recognize you for your efforts, but that doesn't always happen. So along with the goals that you set and the measurement system that you put in place, make sure to create some ways to reward yourself for achieving your goals. Take yourself out to lunch—and ask a good friend to go with you. Mark the achievement in red pen in your calendar, knowing that every time you look at it you'll get a big smile on your face for accomplishing something. Brag about it to a colleague. Use one of your regular meetings to announce your progress to your team. They will applaud. It's okay to toot your own horn every now and then. By the way, it's also okay to ask others for positive feedback: "Tell me something I did well today." You need that, too.

TIP 10. BE HONEST WITH YOURSELF AND HUMBLE WITH OTHERS

We know from our research that credibility is the foundation of leadership, and honesty is at the top of the list of what constituents look for in a leader. What does honesty have to do with learning to lead? Everything. You can't become better at something unless you're able to recognize and accept your strengths and your areas for improvement. In our research we have yet to encounter a leader who scores a perfect 10 on every behavior. We all can improve, and the first step is understanding what most needs to be improved. We don't mean you're supposed to beat yourself up over faults and mistakes; just be intellectually and emotionally honest.

Being honest means that you're willing to admit mistakes, own up to your faults, and be open to suggestions for improvement. It also means that you're accepting of the same in others. We're by no means saying that it's okay for you and others to repeat the same mistake over and over again. The point is simply that neither you nor anyone can improve without being willing to admit to and to accept error as part of the improvement process.

Honesty with yourself and others also produces a level of humility that earns you credibility. People don't respect know-it-alls, especially when they know that the know-it-all doesn't know it all. People like people who show they are human. Admitting mistakes and being open to accepting new ideas and new learning communicates that you are willing to grow. It does something else as well. It promotes a culture of honesty and openness. That's healthy for you and for others.

Hubris is the killer disease in leadership. It's fun to be a leader, gratifying to have influence, and exhilarating to have scores of people cheering your every word. In many all-too-subtle ways, it's easy to be seduced by power and importance. All evil leaders have been infected with the disease of hubris, becoming bloated with an exaggerated sense of self and pursuing their own sinister ends. How then to avoid it?

Humility is the only way to resolve the conflicts and contradictions of leadership. You can avoid excessive pride only if you recognize that you're human and need the help of others, and that's another important reason for leaders being great learners.

Resources

We hope you have found your experience with the Leadership Practices Inventory (LPI) assessment insightful and worthwhile. If you are looking for everyday opportunities to make a small difference in your world, need tools to start or a community to keep inspired, obtain feedback on how you are doing, or implement a leadership development program within your organization, we can help. Here are some of the resources you can draw on as you begin or continue your leadership journey.

Books

Jim and Barry's books include *The Leadership Challenge, Credibility, Encouraging the Heart, The Truth About Leadership, A Leader's Legacy, The Student Leadership Challenge,* and *The Jossey-Bass Academic Administrator's Guide to Exemplary Leadership.*

Workbooks

Jim and Barry believe that an important part of the learning process is practice, practice, practice, so they have created *The Leadership Challenge Workbook, The Encouraging the Heart Workbook, Strengthening Credibility: A Leader's Workbook, The Leadership Challenge Practice Book,* and *The Leadership Challenge Vision Book.* These interactive tools are designed to be used on that proverbial Monday morning when you are faced with a problem or situation and would like to resolve the issue using their framework.

App

The Leadership Challenge Mobile Tool, a smart phone application, is a convenient way to examine and employ The Five Practices of Exemplary Leadership® and the thirty LPI behaviors in your daily life. Features of the app include a seamless request-and-receive feedback process through which overall leadership performance can be tracked and measured, helpful action planning routines, model overview, and an inspirational quote of the day.

Videos

These visual aids to The Leadership Challenge program bring inspiring, real-life examples to the leadership development process. There are multiple video case examples of each of The Five Practices of Exemplary Leadership®.

Workshop

The Leadership Challenge Workshop is a unique, intensive program that consistently receives rave reviews from attendees. It has served as a catalyst for profound leadership transformation in organizations of all sizes and in all industries. The program is highly interactive and stimulating. Participants experience and apply Jim and Barry's leadership model through video cases, workbook activities, group problem-solving tasks, lectures, and outdoor action learning. Quite often we hear workshop attendees describe how The Leadership Challenge is more than a training event and talk about how it changed their lives. It's a bold statement, we know, but we've watched it happen time after time, leader after leader.

Combined, these resources truly make Jim and Barry the most trusted sources for becoming a better leader. To find out more about these products, please visit www.leadershipchallenge .com. If you would like to speak to a leadership consultant about bringing The Leadership Challenge to your organization or team, call 866-888-5159 (toll free).

FURTHER READING

General Leadership

Burlingham, B. *Small Giants: Companies That Choose to Be Great Instead of Big*. New York: Penguin Group, 2005.

Collins, J. *Good to Great: Why Some Companies Make the Leap and Others Don't*. New York: HarperCollins, 2001.

Collins, J. *Great by Choice: Uncertainty, Chaos, and Luck: Why Some Companies Thrive Despite Them All*. New York: HarperCollins, 2011.

Gallos, J. V. (Ed.). *Business Leadership: A Jossey-Bass Reader*. San Francisco: Jossey-Bass, 2003.

Hamel, G. *What Matters Now: How to Win in a World of Relentless Change, Ferocious Competition, and Unstoppable Innovation*. San Francisco: Jossey-Bass, 2012.

Hamm, J. *Unusually Excellent: The Necessary Nine Skills Required for the Practice of Great Leadership*. San Francisco: Jossey-Bass, 2011.

Heifitz, R. A., and Linsky, M. *Leadership on the Line: Staying Alive Through the Dangers of Leading*. Boston: Harvard Business School Press, 2002.

Kawaski, G. *Enchantment: The Art of Changing Hearts, Minds, and Actions*. New York: Portfolio, 2011.

Kouzes, J. M., and Posner, B. Z. *The Truth About Leadership: The No-Fads, Heart-of-the-Matter Facts You Need to Know*. San Francisco: Jossey-Bass, 2010.

Peters, T. *Re-Imagine! Business Excellence in a Disruptive Age*. New York: DK Publishing, Inc., 2003.

Pfeffer, J. *What Were They Thinking?: Unconventional Wisdom About Management*. Boston: Harvard Business School Press, 2007.

Porras, J., Emery, S., and Thompson, M. *Success Built to Last: Creating a Life That Matters.* Upper Saddle River, NJ: Wharton School Publishing, 2006.

Thompson, R. H. *The Offsite: A Leadership Challenge Fable*. San Francisco: Jossey-Bass, 2008.

Model the Way

Block, P. *The Answer to How Is Yes: Acting On What Matters*. San Francisco: Berrett-Koehler, 2002.

Conant, D., and Norgaard, M. *TouchPoints: Creating Powerful Leadership Connections in the Smallest of Moments*. San Francisco: Jossey-Bass, 2011.

DePree, M. *Leadership Is an Art*. New York: Doubleday, 2004.

George, B. *True North: Discover Your Authentic Leadership*. San Francisco: Jossey-Bass, 2007.

Goleman, D. *Social Intelligence: The New Science of Human Relationships*. New York: Bantam, 2006.

Kouzes, J. M., and B. Z. Posner. *Credibility: How Leaders Gain and Lose It, Why People Demand* (2nd ed.). San Francisco: Jossey-Bass, 2011.

Kraemer, H. M. J., Jr. *From Values to Action: The Four Principles of Values-Based Leadership*. San Francisco: Jossey-Bass, 2011.

Maister, D. *Practice What You Preach: What Managers Must Do to Create a High Achievement Culture*. New York: The Free Press, 2001.

Palmer, P. *Let Your Life Speak: Listening to the Voice of Vocation*. San Francisco: Jossey-Bass, 2000.

Pearce, T. *Leading Out Loud: Inspiring Change Through Authentic Communications* (new and revised). San Francisco: Jossey-Bass, 2003.

Rhoads, A., with Shepherdson, N. *Built on Values: Creating an Enviable Culture That Outperforms the Competition*. San Francisco: Jossey-Bass, 2011.

Schein, E. *Organizational Culture and Leadership* (4th ed.). San Francisco: Jossey-Bass, 2010.

Inspire a Shared Vision

Burns, J. M. *Transforming Leadership.* New York: Atlantic Books, 2003.

Clarke, B., and Crossland, R. *The Leader's Voice: How Your Communication Can Inspire Action and Get Results!* New York: SelectBooks, 2002.

Fredrickson, B. L. *Positivity: Groundbreaking Research Reveals How to Embrace the Hidden Strengths of Positive Emotions, Overcome Negativity, and Thrive.* New York: Crown, 2009.

Geary, J. *I Is an Other: The Secret Life of Metaphor and How It Shapes the Way We See the World.* New York: Harper, 2011.

Heath, C., and Heath, D. *Made to Stick: Why Some Ideas Survive and Others Die.* New York: Random House, 2007.

Leider, J., and Shapiro, D. *Whistle While You Work: Heeding Your Life's Calling.* San Francisco: Berrett-Koehler, 2001.

Maxwell, J. C. *Developing the Leader Within You* (rev. ed.). New York: Nelson Books, 2005.

Naisbitt, J. *Mindset: Reset Your Thinking and See the Future.* New York: HarperCollins, 2006.

Pink, D. *Drive: The Surprising Truth About What Motivates Us.* New York: Penguin Group, 2009.

Schuster, J. P. *The Power of Your Past: The Art of Recalling, Recasting, and Reclaiming.* San Francisco: Berrett-Koehler, 2011.

Sinek, S. *Start with Why: How Great Leaders Inspire Everyone to Take Action.* New York: Portfolio, 2010.

Spence, R. M. *It's Not What You Sell, It's What You Stand For: Why Every Extraordinary Business Is Driven by Purpose*. New York: Portfolio, 2010.

Sullenberger, C. B. *Making a Difference: Stories of Vision and Courage from America's Leaders.* New York: William Morrow, 2012.

Ulrich, D., and Ulrich, W. *The Why of Work: How Great Leaders Build Abundant Organizations That Win.* New York: McGraw-Hill, 2010.

Wheatley, M. *Turning to One Another: Simple Conversations to Restore Hope to the Future* (2nd. ed.). San Francisco: Berrett-Koehler, 2009.

Challenge the Process

Amabile, T. A., and Kramer, S. J. *The Progress Principle: Using Small Wins to Ignite Joy, Engagement, and Creativity at Work*. Boston: Harvard Business Review Press, 2011.

Ariely, D. *Predictably Irrational: The Hidden Forces That Shape Our Decisions* (rev. and expanded). New York: HarperCollins, 2009.

Blum, A. *Annapurna: A Woman's Place* (20th ann. ed.). San Francisco: Sierra Club Books, 1998.

Csikszentmihalyi, M. *Flow: The Psychology of Optimal Experience*. New York: Harper, 2008.

Davila, T., Epstein, M. J., and Shelton, R. *Making Innovation Work: How to Manage It, Measure It, and Profit from It*. Upper Saddle River, NJ: Wharton School Publishing, 2006.

Farson, R., and Keyes, R. *Whoever Makes the Most Mistakes Wins: The Paradox of Innovation*. New York: The Free Press, 2002.

Foster, R., and Kaplan, S. *Creative Destruction: Why Companies That Are Built to Last Underperform the Market—and How to Successfully Transform Them*. New York: Currency, 2001.

Gladwell, M. Blink: *The Power of Thinking Without Thinking*. New York: Little, Brown and Company, 2005.

Johnson, S. *Where Good Ideas Come From: The Natural History of Innovation.* New York: Riverhead, 2010.

Kelley, T., with Littman, J. *The Art of Innovation: Lessons in Creativity from IDEO, America's Leading Design Firm*. New York: Currency Doubleday, 2001.

Klein, G. *Intuition at Work: Why Developing Your Gut Instincts Will Make You Better at What You Do*. New York: Currency Doubleday, 2002.

Seligman, M.E.P. *Flourish: A Visionary New Understanding of Happiness and Well-Being.* New York: The Free Press, 2011.

Sims, P. *Little Bets: How Breakthrough Ideas Emerge from Small Discoveries*. New York: The Free Press, 2011.

Yamashita, K., and Spataro, S. *Unstuck: A Tool for Yourself, Your Team, and Your World* (rev. ed.). New York: Portfolio/Penguin Group, 2007.

Zander, R. S., and Zander, B. *The Art of Possibility: Transforming Professional and Personal Life*. New York: Penguin Group, 2002.

Enable Others to Act

Boyatzis, R., and McKee, A. *Resonant Leadership.* Boston: Harvard Business School Press, 2004.

Brooks, D. *The Social Animal: Hidden Sources of Love, Character, and Achievement.* New York: Random House, 2011.

Burchell, M., and Robin, J. *The Great Workplace: How to Build It, How to Keep It, and Why It Matters.* San Francisco: Jossey-Bass, 2011.

Cherniss, C., and Goleman, D. (Eds.). *The Emotionally Intelligent Workplace: How to Select for, Measure, and Improve Emotional Intelligence in Individuals, Groups, and Organizations.* San Francisco: Jossey-Bass, 2001.

Covey, S. M., Merrill, R. R., and Covey, S. R. *The SPEED of Trust: The One Thing That Changes Everything.* New York: The Free Press, 2006.

Farber, S. *Greater Than Yourself: The Ultimate Lesson of True Leadership*. New York: Doubleday, 2009.

Gladwell, M. *The Tipping Point: How Little Things Make a Big Difference.* Boston: Little, Brown and Company, 2000.

Hansen, M. T. *Collaboration: How Leaders Avoid the Traps, Create Unity, and Reap Big Results.* Boston: Harvard Business School Press, 2009.

Hughes, M. M., Patterson, L. B., and Terrell, J. B. *Emotional Intelligence in Action: Training and Coaching Activities for Leaders and Managers.* San Francisco: Pfeiffer, 2005.

Hurley, R. F. *The Decision to Trust: How Leaders Create High-Trust* Organizations. San Francisco: Jossey-Bass, 2012.

Kanter, R. M. *Confidence: How Winning Streaks and Losing Streaks Begin and End.* New York: Crown Business, 2004.

Lencioni, P. M. *The Five Dysfunctions of a Team: A Leadership Fable*. San Francisco: Jossey-Bass, 2002.

Maddi, S. R., and Khoshaba, D. M. *Resilience at Work: How to Succeed No Matter What Life Throws at You.* New York: American Management Association, 2005.

Merchant, N. *The New How: Creating Business Solutions Through Collaborative Strategy.* San Francisco: O'Reilly Media, 2010.

O'Reilly, C., and Pfeffer, J. *Hidden Value: How Great Companies Achieve Extraordinary Results with Ordinary People*. Boston: Harvard Business School Press, 2000.

Shockley-Zalabak, P. S., Morreale, S. and Hackman, M. *Building the High-Trust Organization: Strategies for Supporting Five Key Dimensions of Trust.* San Francisco: Jossey-Bass, 2010.

Wiseman, L. *Multipliers: How the Best Leaders Make Everyone Smarter.* New York: HarperCollins, 2010.

Encourage the Heart

Achor, S. *The Happiness Advantage: The Seven Principles of Positive Psychology That Fuel Success and Performance at Work*. New York: Crown Books, 2010.

Blanchard, K., and Bowles, S. *High Five! The Magic of Working Together*. New York: William Morrow, 2000.

Blanchard, K., Lacinak, T., Tompkins, C., and Ballard, J. *Whale Done! The Power of Positive Relationships*. New York: The Free Press, 2002.

Cameron, K. S., Dutton, J. E., and Quinn, R. E. (Eds.). *Positive Organizational Scholarship: Foundations of a New Discipline.* San Francisco: Berrett-Koehler, 2003.

Deal, T. E., and Key, M. K. *Corporate Celebrations: Play, Purpose, and Profit at Work*. San Francisco: Berrett-Koehler, 1998.

Goffee, R., and Jones, G. *Why Should Anyone Be Led by YOU?* Boston: Harvard Business School Press, 2006.

Gostick, A., and Elton, C. *All In: How the Best Managers Create a Culture of Belief and Drive Big Results*. New York: The Free Press, 2012

Kaye, B., and Jordan-Evans, S. *Love 'Em or Lose 'Em: Getting Good People to Stay* (4th ed.). San Francisco: Berrett-Koehler, 2008.

Kouzes, J. M., and Posner, B. Z. *Encouraging the Heart: A Leader's Guide to Rewarding and Recognizing Others*. San Francisco: Jossey-Bass, 2003.

Rath, T., and Clifton, D. O. *How Full Is Your Bucket? Positive Strategies for Work and Life*. New York: Gallup Press, 2004.

Rath, T., and Harter, J. *Well-Being: The Five Essential Elements*. New York: Gallup Press, 2010.

Seligman, M. E. Flourish: *A Visionary New Understanding of Happiness and Well-Being*. New York: The Free Press, 2011.

Ventrice, C. *Make Their Day! Employee Recognition That Works*. San Francisco: Berrett-Koehler, 2003.

ABOUT THE AUTHORS

Jim Kouzes and Barry Posner have been working together for more than thirty years, studying leaders, researching leadership, conducting leadership development seminars, and serving as leaders themselves in various capacities. They are coauthors of the award-winning, best-selling book *The Leadership Challenge.* Since its first edition in 1987, *The Leadership Challenge* has sold more than two million copies worldwide and is available in more than twenty-two languages. It has won numerous awards, including the Critics' Choice Award from the nation's book review editors and the James A. Hamilton Hospital Administrators' Book of the Year Award, and was selected as one of the top ten books on leadership in Covert and Sattersten's *Top 100 Business Books of All Time.*

Jim and Barry have coauthored more than a dozen other award-winning leadership books, including *Credibility: How Leaders Gain and Lose It, Why People Demand It; The Truth about Leadership: The No-Fads, Heart-of-the-Matter Facts You Need to Know; A Leader's Legacy; Encouraging the Heart; The Student Leadership Challenge;* and *The Academic Administrator's Guide to Exemplary Leadership.* They also developed the highly acclaimed Leadership Practices Inventory (LPI), a 360-degree questionnaire for assessing leadership behavior, which is one of the most widely used leadership assessment instruments in the world, along with The Student LPI. The Five Practices of Exemplary Leadership® model which they developed has been the basis of more than five hundred doctoral dissertations and academic research projects (a summary of these are available on the web at www.theleadershipchallenge.com/research).

Among the honors and awards that Jim and Barry have received is the American Society for Training and Development's highest award for their Distinguished Contribution to Workplace Learning and Performance. They have been named Management/Leadership Educators of the Year by the International Management Council; ranked by *Leadership Excellence* magazine in the top twenty on its list of the Top 100 Thought Leaders; named among the Top 50 Leadership Coaches in the nation (according to *Coaching for Leadership*); and listed among *HR Magazine*'s Most Influential International Thinkers.

Jim and Barry are frequent speakers, and each has conducted leadership development programs for organizations such as Apple, Applied Materials, ARCO, AT&T, Australia Institute of Management, Australia Post, Bank of America, Bose, Charles Schwab, Cisco Systems, Clorox, Community Leadership Association, Conference Board of Canada, Consumers Energy, Deloitte Touche, Dorothy Wylie Nursing Leadership Institute, Dow Chemical, Egon Zehnder International, Federal Express, Genentech, Google, Gymboree, HP, IBM, Jobs DR-Singapore, Johnson & Johnson, Kaiser Foundation Health Plans and Hospitals, Intel, Itau Unibanco, L. L. Bean, Lawrence Livermore National Labs, Lucile Packard Children's Hospital, Merck, Motorola, NetApp, Northrop Grumman, Novartis, Nvidia, Oakwood Housing, Oracle, Petronas, Roche Bioscience, Siemens, 3M, Toyota, United Way, USAA, Verizon, VISA, the Walt Disney Company, and Westpac. They have lectured at over sixty college and university campuses.

Jim Kouzes is the Dean's Executive Fellow of Leadership, Leavey School of Business, at Santa Clara University, and lectures on leadership around the world to corporations, governments, and nonprofits. He is a highly regarded leadership scholar and an experienced executive; the *Wall Street Journal* cited him as one of the twelve best executive educators in the United States. In 2010, Jim received the Thought Leadership Award from the Instructional Systems Association, the most prestigious award given by the trade association of training and development industry providers. In 2006, Jim was presented with the Golden Gavel, the highest honor awarded by Toastmasters International. Jim served as president, CEO, and chairman of the Tom Peters Company from 1988 through 1999, and prior to that led the Executive Development Center at Santa Clara University (1981–1987). Jim founded the Joint Center for Human Services Development at San Jose State University (1972–1980) and was on the staff of the School of Social Work, University of Texas. His career in training and development began in 1969 when he conducted seminars for Community Action Agency staff and volunteers in the war on poverty. Following graduation from Michigan State University (BA degree with honors in political science), he served as a Peace Corps volunteer (1967–1969). Jim can be reached at jim@kouzes.com.

Barry Posner is Accolti Professor of Leadership at the Leavey School of Business, Santa Clara University, where he served as dean of the school for twelve years (1997–2009). He has been a distinguished visiting professor at Hong Kong University of Science and Technology, Sabanci University (Istanbul), and the University of Western Australia. At Santa Clara he has received the President's Distinguished Faculty Award, the School's Extraordinary Faculty Award, and several other teaching and academic honors. An internationally renowned scholar and educator, Barry is author or coauthor of more than a hundred research and practitioner-focused articles. He currently serves on the editorial advisory boards for *Leadership and Organizational Development* and *The International Journal of Servant-Leadership.* In 2011, he received the Outstanding Scholar Award from the *Journal of Management Inquiry.*

Barry received his BA (with honors) in political science from the University of California, Santa Barbara; his MA in public administration from The Ohio State University; and his Ph.D. in organizational behavior and administrative theory from the University of Massachusetts, Amherst. Having consulted with a wide variety of public and private sector organizations around the globe, Barry also works at a strategic level with a number of community-based and professional organizations, currently sitting on the board of directors of EMQ FamiliesFirst and the Global Women's Leadership Network. He has served previously on the boards of the American Institute of Architects (AIA), Big Brothers/Big Sisters of Santa Clara County, Center for Excellence in Nonprofits, Junior Achievement of Silicon Valley and Monterey Bay, Public Allies, San Jose Repertory Theater, Sigma Phi Epsilon Fraternity, and several start-up companies. Barry can be reached at bposner@scu.edu.

More information about Jim and Barry and their work, research, and services can be found at www.theleadershipchallenge.com.

NOTES

NOTES

NOTES

NOTES

NOTES

NOTES

NOTES

NOTES

NOTES

NOTES

NOTES

NOTES